LOVE AND SEX CONNECTIVITY:
Is it A Choice or Necessity (The Tonic of Soul)?

Rolando Gleeson

Table of Contents

Chapter 1

LOVE AND SEX CONNECTION

Will our health be in balance if we don't have sex? Exists a right and wrong about sex?

Every society has laws governing who is allowed to have sex with whom, when, and where.

Love is a sexually motivated attraction. From the highest virtue or good habit to the most profound interpersonal attachment, love comprises a variety of powerful and pleasant emotional and mental states, from the most straightforward pleasure. Sex (defined as the union of the sexes) develops via sexual activity when a man and a woman become ONE (Two Bodies and Two Hearts result in ONE SOUL).

At this point, they become one on a psychological, spiritual, emotional, and bodily level.

Sex should undoubtedly be an expression of love, and the deeper the love, the more intense the sex should be. The more passionate the love, the more fulfilling the sex. Please take notice that sex without love is degrading and leads to emptiness.

What characteristics define real love?

- Distinctive: Love someone for who they are.

- Absolute: Love with all of your heart, mind, and soul.

- Constant: Remain consistent and steady.

- Eternal: After death and forever.

The person you are dating must have each of the qualities listed above. Think about your capacity for love based on:

- Intensity: How long can you keep loving someone?

- How long can a relationship be sustained?

- Range: To what extent can love to render a person insane?

- Purity: Think about what motivates you to keep up connections.

There is a certain connotation when we say that two people are making love rather than engaging in sex. Are there any distinctions, though?

We can all agree that the majority of women between the ages of 21 and 60 believed that to find the greatest amount of satisfaction in both sex relationships and marriage, love was necessary.

Beyond only the emotional benefits, loving a sexual partner has other benefits as well. For the great majority of the female participants in the research, love increased the enjoyment of the sexual activity. The majority of women have drawn a relationship between love and sex, and they think that love improves the pleasure factor of sex.

Women who cherished their sexual partners reported feeling less constrained and being more open to sexual experimentation. Women who experience love could have more sexual autonomy because they not only trust their partners but also believe that having sex is acceptable when love is present.

Chapter 2

HOW IMPORTANT IS SEX IN A RELATIONSHIP

The fact is that there isn't a universal solution to this. Because everyone is unique, what is significant to some people may not be at all significant to others. In the end, it comes down to your values, sexual preferences, and relationship dynamics. Sex isn't always required, however, for some people. Without having intercourse with their spouses, many individuals enjoy happy, meaningful, and healthy love relationships.

People may not want to or may not have sex for a variety of reasons. This could comprise:

1. A lack of libido is sometimes referred to as a "sex drive."

2. Suffering from a primary medical issue, such as persistent discomfort.

3. Desiring longer relationships before engaging in sexual activity.

4. Being single and wishing, by your beliefs, to forego having sex before marriage.

This does not necessarily imply that the relationship will be harmful, however. It also doesn't always mean that your spouse doesn't appreciate or love you! Having sex is a crucial component of love relationships, at least for some people like myself. Many individuals want a sexual relationship with the person they are dating. There is a spectrum of sexuality.

While all sexual individuals feel sexual desire, asexual persons seldom do (and often don't have sex, but each person is different). We all have various approaches to sex since there is such a wide range in our capacity for sexual attraction and our sentiments about sex, but no method is incorrect.

You will all get to choose how you want your partner to remain with you forever. There are several reasons why your relationship may include sexual intimacy. For instance:

1. It could be a chance for you to become closer to your spouse.

2. You may use the occasion to express your love and affection for your partner.

3. If you often engage in sexual activity with an attractive man, you could feel more confident in your relationship.

4. It can just be enjoyable and enjoyable to be with that naughty guy who is kind to your lovely soul.

5. You could be attempting to conceive.

Regular sexual activity has a variety of advantages from a medical standpoint. Do you even realize that having sex has many advantages other than just being enjoyable? There are a variety of reasons why having sex is excellent for your body, mind, and relationships. Three categories might be used to analyze this:

- ***First Category***

1. Emotional Reasons: Many individuals have emotional reasons for engaging in sexual activity. Sex has several emotional advantages, such as:
2. It could boost your self-confidence.

3. It could facilitate a nice connection between you and your body.
4. It could strengthen your relationship with your lover and serve as a means of showing them your affection.
5. It may help you relax.

- ***Second Category***

Goal-Based Reasons: To have a child, raise one's social standing (by, say, becoming popular), or exact retribution.

- ***Third Category***

    1. Physical Reasons: Even your body and your wellness may benefit from sex. For instance, according to some studies, sex may: Boost immunological function. According to my

earlier research, those who engaged in sex more often had stronger immune systems.

2. Serve as a sort of easy workout. My earlier experiment also showed that having sex gives us a surprisingly terrific exercise.

3. Boost cardiovascular health. Regular intercourse may lower the chance of getting heart disease, according to a psychologist.

4. Boost cognitive performance. A buddy of mine who is a scientist discovered in 2016 that those who were sexually active between the ages of 50 and 90 had superior memories.

5. Alleviate headaches. Over time, it has been shown that SEX may

help people with migraines or cluster headaches.

Men Consider Sex Important

Many people see having sex as a crucial act between two committed individuals. Men also find SEXUAL INTIMACY to be most pleasurable inside a committed RELATIONSHIP, just like most women do. One explanation is that long-term PARTNERS are more adept at pleasing one another than STRANGERS.
Even so, do you know why guys sleep after having sex? This is caused by PROLACTIN.

The sole known use of prolactin in humans is to stimulate the production of breast milk. Prolactin is a hormone produced in the pituitary gland at the base of the brain.

Men also have prolactin, but it has no recognized purpose. Prolactin injections cause animals to get fatigued right away since their levels are normally greater during sleep. The production of hormones during orgasm most likely leads males to feel sleepy since there is a significant correlation between PROLACTIN and SLEEP.

Is Missing Someone a Sign of Love?

When you begin to fall in love with someone, you naturally want to spend as much time with them as you can and miss them when you are away. But this sense of missing someone is not always a sign of romantic love. It could be the first manifestations of a crush, an attraction, desire, or simple infatuation.

His willingness to give you his best and his things are one indication that he loves you.

He will unburden himself and want you to be engaged in every aspect of his life, but many women today take this for granted, and I too have suffered as a result. He will also reveal to you his deepest secrets that he cannot discuss with anyone else.

This only implies that those who engage in sex may also experience progress in other areas. It does not imply that those who refrain from engaging in sex would always suffer emotionally or physically.

Keep in mind that these advantages shouldn't be used to force individuals to have sex if they don't want to. It also demonstrates how SEX predicts AFFECTION, and AFFECTION predicts how often people engage in sexual behavior. That is to say, MORE sex just encourages more sex. Therefore, the greatest course of action for having sex is to HAVE MORE SEX! Although it may seem foolish, it will eventually help your whole sexual life and sex drive.

Do you even realize that intimacy with your spouse may exist outside of sexual relations? Although SEX may be a wonderful type of intimacy, we often confuse it with being intimate. There are many other ways to be close to someone. For instance, affectionate TOUCH might be a wonderful technique to become close. The following are examples of NON-SEXUAL physical intimacy: cuddling, holding hands, massages, and sensual kissing.

Chapter 3

SEXUAL COMPATIBILITY

When one partner believes that having sex is necessary for a healthy relationship but the other does not, dealing with this scenario may be challenging.

In the same vein, although it may be challenging to handle if one person has a strong libido while the other does not (Big Issue!), Communication may be quite beneficial.

- **Why Sex and Love are necessity and not a Choice**

The source of both love and sexual desire is the same. Sex is made more fulfilling by love. Love brings comfort and assurance to the mix. Love Makes Sex More Meaningful. People attempt in vain to fill the void left by love with sex. Relationships that don't have sex struggle or end in failure. Having sex in a loving relationship makes love feelings more intense.

Additionally, loving couples have sex more often. The sentiments of love that the couple has for one another get stronger when they are both involved and frequently partake in sexual activity. This relates to the first justification given and how your brain functions. It's also the reason why sexless couples see a decline in romantic sentiments. If the discomfort is not caused by a physical condition, you have not yet met your true soul mate since a pussy would naturally cuddle when it first meets its owner.

Despite society's best efforts, it is difficult to exclude love from the sexual experience. Sex and love are related. You can have sex without being in love, but that won't end well in the long run. Sex without love, on the other hand, invites a host of challenges and emotional turbulence. Similar to this, at some point, sex will be involved in a long-term love engagement. You cannot succeed long-term by doing one without the other. This is similar to a car without an engine that uses oil.

Many individuals often fail to see the differences between the two quite distinct activities of making love and having sex, whether they are men or women. Sex is an instinctual and bio-mechanical act that everyone can do, as stated in Thought Catalog.

Making love, on the other hand, is seen as a sensuous, leisurely, and non-objective act that allows us the chance to feel the metaphysical being of oneness and is regarded as a kind of art in and of itself. As a result, little of each should be present in a healthy love relationship and a satisfying sexual life.

According to the World Health Organization (WHO), sexual health is a state of mental, physical, and social well-being about one's sexuality. It necessitates having a positive and respectful perspective on sexuality and romantic relationships, as well as the capacity to enjoy sexual experiences free from coercion, violence, and prejudice.

The meaning of sex or sexual activity varies from person to person, but one thing is certain: most people find sex or sexual activity to be a healthy and natural activity that they enjoy and find significance in their particular manner. Additionally, one may choose to do this act for a variety of reasons, such as passion, closeness, boredom, relief, power, expectation fulfillment, childbearing, expressing love, seeking comfort, etc.

There is no more personal act than allowing another person to enter a private bodily part to share pleasure, thus we should be conscious that this act is believed to be one of sharing and closeness.

Even though the phrases "having sex" and "making love" are sometimes used interchangeably and even while making love frequently includes sexual activity, they do not always refer to the same thing. When two people make love, their degrees of vulnerability are rather high. This often happens as a consequence of people exchanging words and feelings that they may not have done previously.

Risk and reward are factors that come into play when both people prefer to let their guard down. One feels particularly connected to their spouse when in a loving relationship and finds it difficult to picture other times occurring without them.

On the other hand, while vulnerability still plays a part when you are having sex with someone, it takes a different form. In particular, one can worry that the sex won't be satisfying or lose the necessary chemistry. People who understand the difference also understand that, whether it entails the occasional missionary posture or more daring explorations, making love requires both parties to be completely themselves, honest, and raw, as they are daily. Couples can relax and make love without feeling any pressure or limitation about their sexual demands or desires because of their shared love and understanding.

Having sex does not always include genuine feelings and emotions and people may allow themselves to not be the person they are on a daily, as noted on Your Tango. One may try out all kinds of sexual desires and expose a different side of themselves that they may never actually show publically. You may also be expressing some hidden personality traits through the act of having sex.

When love is not in the picture but merely getting sexual pleasure, saying goodbye is never a problem and one may be able to move on without necessarily looking for commitment from the other side involved. However, this is not always the case when you are making love with a person with whom you have found a connection. Lovemaking puts more at stake than getting and giving sexual pleasure, like your feelings, emotions, and deepest thoughts that are shared during this act.

This is why saying goodbye is not always something easily done and both partners feel more committed to each other. If you thought that the only benefit of sex was, well, pleasure, here's some news for you. Making love is good for adults. And making love regularly is even better.

Sex is evergreen, hot and all things nice. There aren't enough words to describe the exhilarating moment of getting intimate with your partner. When lips and bodies touch, some fireworks and explosions make you feel like you're at the top of the world. With love, trust and understanding come intimacy and sex. This extremely intimate act not only gives you and your partner intense pleasure but also helps you sleep well, relieve stress, and release happy endorphins within the body. And not to forget, burns a ton of calories!

Chapter 4

BUILDING EMOTIONAL INTIMACY

Sex is not merely about physical intimacy. It helps to strengthen the emotional bond between the two partners. For any relationship to be successful, it's important that the people involved are emotionally on the same page and having sex is a great way to build that emotional intimacy. Sex is not expected to be detachable from Love since it serves as a tonic for soul survival through the following:

- Improves cardiovascular health

A recent study says that men who have sex more than twice a week, have a lesser risk of getting a heart attack, than men who had sex less than once a month.

- Increases immunity

Regular lovemaking increases the level of the immune-boosting antibody immunoglobulin A (IgA), which in turn makes your body stronger against illnesses like the common cold and fever.

- Reduces stress

Stressed out with work or family problems? Don't let it affect your performance in the bedroom. Not only will having sex improve your mood, but a study has also proven that folks, who indulge in regular bedroom activities can handle stress better and are happier people.

- Relieves pain

If you're using a headache as an excuse to not make love, stop doing that. Have sex instead, because, when you're about to have an orgasm, the level of the hormone oxytocin increases by five times. This endorphin reduces aches and pains.

- Promotes longevity

When one has an orgasm, a hormone called dehydroepiandrosterone is released. This improves immunity, repairs tissue, and keeps the skin healthy. Men, who have at least two orgasms a week, live longer than men who have sex just once every few weeks.

- Increases blood circulation

Because your heart rate increases when you have sex, fresh blood is supplied to your organs and cells. While used blood is removed, the body also expels toxins and other materials that cause you to feel tired.

- You sleep better

The sleep that you get just after you have made love will be much more relaxed. Getting a good night's sleep will make you feel alert and overall healthy.

- Improves overall fitness

If you find going to the gym mundane or working out at home a task, here's another way to help you lose the flab and keep in shape. Regular sex will do wonders for your waistline. Half an hour of lovemaking burns more than 80 calories.

- Increases levels of Oestrogen and testosterone

In men, the hormone testosterone is what makes them more passionate in the sack. Not only will it make you feel way better in bed, but it also improves your muscles and bones, keeps your heart healthy, and keeps a check on your cholesterol. In women, on the other hand, the hormone estrogen protects them against heart disease and also determines a woman's body scent.

- Reduces the chances of getting depression

Just any other form of exercise, sex also prompts the brain to release feel-good chemicals, which increases the levels of happy hormones. These chemicals also help increase the levels of serotonin, which acts as a neurotransmitter and is one of the key antidepressant chemicals in the body. This, in turn, helps reduce the chances of getting depression.

- Feel better throughout the day

According to research, people who had sex in the morning coped better with their daily stress better and even sailed through the day in a good mood. Thanks to all the happy hormones produced after a session of sex, couples are armed with a smile to all the challenges that life throws at them daily.

How is Sex to A Man

For many, sex is a very important act between two committed people. And just like most women, men find sexual intimacy to be most satisfying within a committed relationship. One reason is that long-term partners know how to please one another better than strangers do. Most guys feel as though they're the ones who always initiate sex. But they also like to be pursued and wish their partner would take the lead more often. Don't be shy about letting your guy know you're in the mood. Initiating sex some of the time may lead to a higher level of satisfaction for both of you.

Guys Aren't Always Up for Sex

Men, much to many women's surprise, aren't always in the mood for sex. Just like women, men are often stressed by the demands of work, family, and paying the bills. And stress is a big libido crusher. When a guy says, "not tonight," it doesn't mean they have lost interest in you. They just mean they don't want to have sex right then.

Men Like Pleasing Their Partner

Your pleasure is important to your man. But they won't know what you want unless you tell them. Too many women feel uncomfortable talking about what they like and don't like. If you can tell them clearly in a way that doesn't bruise their ego, they'll listen. Because they know they'll feel good if you feel good.

Guys Get Performance Anxiety

Most men get performance anxiety on occasion, especially as they age. Your guy may worry about their body, technique, and stamina. If you can help them learn to relax and stay focused on the pleasures of the moment, sex will become less stressful.

Men May Stray When their Needs Aren't Met

If a man doesn't feel loved and appreciated in their relationship, they may turn elsewhere for satisfaction. For one man, that may mean burying themselves in work. Another may develop a fixation on sports or video games. And some men cheat. To avoid this, partners need to work together to meet each other's needs.

Most men realize there's a lot to lose if a long-term relationship goes sour -- not just each other's company, but the entire life you've built together. If you're willing to work to strengthen your marriage, chances are your man will be, too.

Chapter 5

EXERCISES PROMOTING SEX

Getting physical with your spouse might increase your enjoyment of each other. Blood flow to your nether regions may be increased by engaging in any activity that causes your heart to beat quicker and your breathing to become more labored, such as cycling or brisk jogging.

You are aware of the benefits of exercise on your health. Your sexual skill, suppleness, and endurance may all benefit greatly from working out three to four times each week. Perform some push-ups, sit-ups, and crunches to enhance your sex life. By strengthening, these muscle-building workouts may improve sex.

Swimming

Swimming is good for your sex life in addition to your physical health and well-being. Along with toning your physique, enhancing heart health, and boosting your energy levels, swimming may increase your desire and sexual performance. Because the water supports the body, it is a fantastic method to start exercising again after surgery, an accident, a heart attack, or if you have a condition that affects your mobility or ability to exercise.

Frog Pose

Exercise physiologist Liz Neporent of NYC claims that this movement will increase your flexibility while making love. Your inner thighs, groin, and hips are stretched during this challenging hip opener. Additionally, tension is released, which may be quite disruptive in bed.

Keep your ankles in line with your knees and your knees bent. Extend the sides of your toes. Placing your palms together or on the ground, take a seat on your forearms with your elbows tucked behind your shoulders.

Additionally, you may put your chin or forehead on the ground while extending your hands forward.

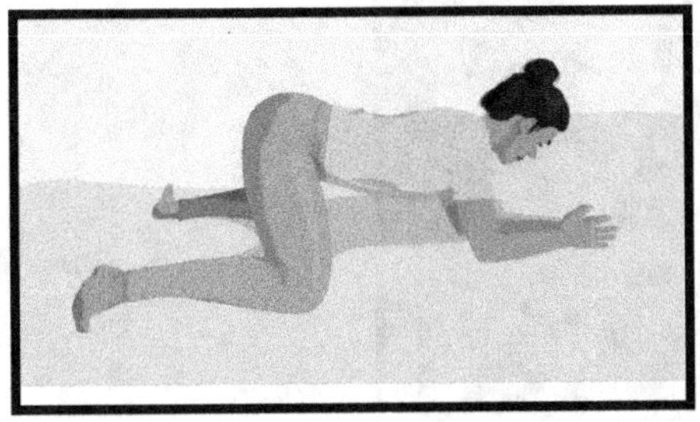

Hinge

Neporent advises the hinge as a way to support oneself in a "favorable posture" without your back or legs wearing out. Repeat by bending your back at a 45-degree angle before standing back up. The action has a lot of staying power while being understated.

Simply described, the hip hinge action involves a modest knee bend, a straight back, and a forward lean that forces your hips backward. Consider it a more strenuous curtsey when your hamstrings and quadriceps are stretched. This action is entirely powered by the hips.

Kegels

Kegel increases blood flow to the vagina and pelvic floor, which may aid in arousal and lubrication. Many women want surgery because they believe their vagina is not as tight as it once was after giving birth. By relaxing your vaginal muscles, which allows your vagina to be more open, kegel exercises may also help you have a healthier and more enjoyable sex life. If you have discomfort during sexual activity, pelvic examinations, or both, this is beneficial. enhancing the flow of blood to your pelvic floor and genital area.

Ladies, if you put your finger in your vagina and squeeze, you should feel a tugging up. Your penis will rise, men. The pelvic floor muscles, which support the uterus, bladder, small intestine, and rectum, are strengthened with kegel exercises.

How to Kegel: Start by laying down or sitting comfortably in a chair. calmly inhale. Exhale, tighten the pelvic floor for 5 seconds, then let it relax for 5 seconds. Ten times in total. allowing your vagina to be more open by letting your vaginal muscles relax. If you have discomfort during sexual activity, this is beneficial.

Plank

The deepest layer of your abdominal muscles (transversus abdominis), as well as your upper arms, thighs, and buttocks, may all be strengthened with this exercise. These muscles aid in stabilizing you so that you may remain close to your spouse at crucial moments. Once every day, work your way up to 60 seconds or more. Try balancing on your knees if staying on your toes is too difficult.

Planks offer your arms the endurance they need for on-top postures like a missionary.

Cat/Cow Stretch

A simple yoga warm-up that stretches the hip flexors and spine is the cat and cow position. Start with your back flat and on your hands and knees. Consider this yoga stance as an additional example of foreplay. It straightens your spine, aids in establishing a regular breathing pattern, and enhances attention, which keeps your mind present. Move in a continuous stream, inhaling fully with each rounding up (the cow portion) and exhaling fully with each arching downward (the cat part).

Better Together (Run at a Pace)

Make an exercise date with your significant other since couples who work out together remain together. According to studies, strenuous exercises like jogging and brisk walking calm you and produce endorphins, which might improve sexual function. Even if you don't know the status of both of your STDs, you should still wear a condom and continue to practice all the other healthy immune-boosting behaviors, such as eating well, being active, getting enough sleep, and staying up to date on your vaccines.

Sex Boosting Libido

Your libido will increase and sex will become better if you have it. According to her, having sex increases vaginal lubrication, blood flow, and suppleness in women, all of which improve the pleasure and desire for sex.

Sex Improves Women's Bladder Control

About 30% of women may have incontinence at some time in their life; preventing it requires having a healthy pelvic floor. Good sex is similar to a pelvic floor muscle exercise. Having an orgasm causes those muscles to contract, which strengthens them.

Sex Lowers Blood Pressure

It has been discovered that having sex—and not just masturbating— decreases systolic blood pressure.

Sex Counts as Exercise

A particularly effective type of exercise is sex. Five calories per minute are burned during sexual activity, four more than during movie viewing. It hits you with a one-two punch by raising your heart rate and working different muscles. So go to work! To make time for it regularly, you may even wish to empty your calendar. Similar to exercising, being consistent may assist enhance the advantages.

Sex Lowers Heart Attack Risk

A satisfying sexual life is heart-healthy. Sex helps maintain a healthy balance between your levels of testosterone and estrogen in addition to being a wonderful method to increase heart rate. You start to develop several issues, including osteoporosis and possibly heart disease, when one of those is low. More sexual activity might be beneficial. According to one research, males who had sex at least twice a week had a 50% lower risk of dying from heart disease.

Sex Lessens Pain

Try to have an orgasm before taking aspirin. Pain may be numb by orgasm. A hormone is released during sexual activity that helps lower pain tolerance. It also works with stimulation without orgasm. Many women have informed us that genital self-stimulation helps lessen menstrual cramps, arthritic pain, and in some instances even headaches. We have discovered that vaginal stimulation can block chronic back and leg discomfort.

Sex May Make Prostate Cancer Less Likely

Going all out might prevent prostate cancer. According to research that was published in the Journal of the American Medical Association, men who ejaculated often (at least 21 times per month) had a lower risk of developing prostate cancer. To gain from this advantage, you don't require a partner: Masturbation, nocturnal emission, and sexual activity were all included. It's debatable if the study's findings were influenced solely by sex. Risk factors for cancer are many. More sexual activity, though, won't harm.

Sex Improves Sleep

After sex, you could fall asleep more rapidly, and for good cause. The hormone prolactin, which causes feelings of relaxation and drowsiness after sex, is produced after an orgasm.

Sex Eases Stress

Being close to your spouse might help you feel less anxious and stressed. Hugging and touching might cause your body's "feel-good hormone" to be released. A brain chemical that activates your brain's pleasure and reward system is released during sexual excitement. Your happiness and self-esteem may both be increased by sex and closeness. It is a prescription for both a healthy and a happy existence.

9 798360 614050